Lennox Lewis

Mike Wilson

Published in association with The Basic Skills Agency

Hodder Murray

A MEMBER OF THE HODDER HEADLINE GROUP

Acknowledgements
Cover: Doug Pensinger/Allsport

Photos: pp 2, 25 © John Gichigi/Allsport; p 4 © Reuters New Media Inc./Corbis; p 9 © Gray Mortimore/Allsport; p 15 © Al Bello/Allsport; p 20 © 'PA' Photo/EPA; p 22 © AP Photo/Laura Ranch; p 27 © Michael Stephens/PA Photos.

Every effort has been made to trace copyright holders of material reproduced in this book. Any rights not acknowledged will be acknowledged in subsequent printings if notice is given to the publisher.

Orders: please contact Bookpoint Ltd, 130 Milton Park, Abingdon, Oxon OX14 4SB. Telephone (44) 01235 827720, Fax: (44) 01235 400454. Lines are open from 9.00–6.00, Monday to Saturday, with a 24 hour message answering service. You can also order through our website: www.hodderheadline.co.uk.

British Library Cataloguing in Publication Data
A catalogue record for this title is available from The British Library

ISBN-10: 0 340 87596 8
ISBN-13: 978 0 340 87596 4

First published 2001
This edition published 2003
Impression number   10 9 8 7 6 5 4 3 2
Year   2007 2006 2005

Copyright © 2001 Mike Wilson

Typeset by SX Composing DTP, Rayleigh, Essex.
Printed in Great Britain for Hodder Murray, a division of Hodder Education, 338 Euston Road, London NW1 3BH by The Bath Press Ltd, Bath.

Contents

1 Heavyweight Champion of the World

Las Vegas.
13 November 1999.

Two men fight
for the title
Heavyweight Champion of the World.

Evander Holyfield is American.
Lennox Lewis is British.

The two men met
ten months before
in March 1999.
That fight was a draw.

This time
there has to be a winner.

In November 1999, Lennox Lewis finally got to prove to
Evander Holyfield who the better boxer was.

After 12 rounds,
the judges give the fight to Lennox Lewis.

The 6ft 5, 18-stone boxer
got what he came for.

He's proved to the world
that he's the best there is.

Lennox Lewis is the first British
Heavyweight Champion
for 100 years.

How did he do it?

Lennox Lewis with his belts when he became Heavyweight Champion of the World.

2 Born fighter

September 2, 1965.

Lennox was born in London.

His mother, Violet,
worked in a hospital.
Lennox never knew his father.
It didn't really bother him.

When he was little,
Lennox wanted to be a fireman.

He was always good at sport.
He liked football and basketball.
And boxing.

He was a good fighter.
Even as a boy, he was big.
Bigger than the other boys.

When he got in a fight,
he always won.

Once,
Lennox was expelled from school
for punching another boy.

In 1972,
Violet moved to Canada.
She went looking for work.
For a better life.

Lennox stayed in London
with family.

Then, in 1977,
he joined his mother
in Canada.

He was 12 years old.

It took time to settle in.
Lennox got into lots more fights!

One day
his head teacher told Lennox:

'I'm tired of telling you off
for fighting!
You have to learn
how to control your aggression.
Go and try boxing.'

That was how Lennox started boxing.

He went to a local gym,
started hanging round,
watching the other boys fight.

Then he had a go himself.

He got punched in the face
a few times.

But Lennox was hooked.
At last he'd found what he was good at.

3 Early Rounds

At first,
Lennox didn't make a living
from boxing.
He was an amateur.

He won 75 of his 82
amateur fights.
58 of the wins were knock-outs.

Then in 1988,
he won a gold medal
at the Olympic Games
in Seoul, Korea.

Lennox Lewis won a gold medal at the 1988 Olympic games.

4 Professional Boxer

After winning a gold medal,
Lennox went professional.

He won his next 25 fights.
Most of them were knock-outs
in the first few rounds.

He beat a boxer called Andrew Golota
in just 95 seconds.

'I just wanted to beat him
before he could commit any fouls!'
he said.

In 1992, Lennox beat 'Razor' Ruddock
in two rounds
to win the WBC title.

Then he met Oliver McCall.
It was in Wembley Arena
in September 1994.

McCall knocked him down
with a right hook,
in the second round.

It was the only time
Lennox has ever been stopped
in a fight.
Lennox waited three years
to get his own back.

In February 1997,
he met Oliver McCall again.

For three rounds,
Lennox was on top.

By then, McCall had had enough.
He turned his back on Lennox.
He walked away, round the ring.
He refused to fight.

In the end,
the ref stopped the fight
in the fifth round.
Lennox won back his WBC title.

His next fight
was a bit of a joke as well.

In July 1997,
Lennox met Henry Akinwande.
He was from Nigeria.

Akinwande was a good boxer,
but Lennox was too much for him.

In round one,
Akinwande stopped boxing.
He just held on to Lennox,
trying to stop the punishment.

Time after time,
he was told to stop holding
and start fighting.
In the end,
the ref stopped the fight
in round five.

'What can you do,' asked Lennox,
'when you get in the ring,
and all the man wants to do
is hold you?'

Akinwande was fined £1 million,
but later it was paid back.

5 The Best

Lennox was WBC World Heavyweight Champion,
but he still had to prove
he was the best.

He wanted to fight Mike Tyson
and beat him.

And he wanted to win
the other two boxing World titles:
the WBA and the IBF.

If Lennox beat Mike Tyson,
he'd hold all three World titles,
he'd be a real World Champion.
No question.

But Tyson would not fight Lennox.
His manager paid Lennox off
and the fight never happened.

So Lennox met Evander Holyfield.

By now Holyfield was WBA and IBF Champion.
He had beaten Mike Tyson twice.
In the second fight,
Tyson had bitten his ear off,
but Holyfield still won!

So if Lennox beat Holyfield,
he'd be The Man.
No question.

Lennox and Holyfield met in New York
in March 1999.

Holyfield was 37,
three years older than Lennox,
but he was a bigger hitter.
And he was better fighting up close.

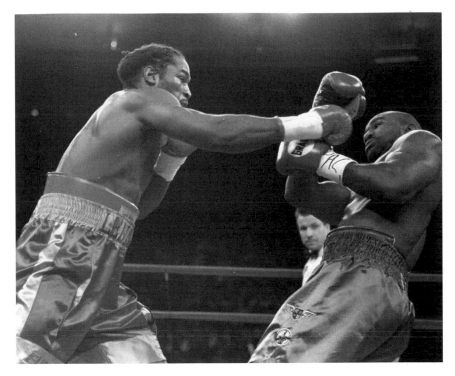

Not everyone agreed with the result of the fight between
Lennox Lewis and Evander Holyfield.

So for 12 rounds,
Lennox kept him at arm's length
with his left jab.
Then he'd hit him
with his big overhand right.

He outboxed Holyfield all night,
in almost every round.

But at the end of the fight,
the three judges said it was a draw.
No-one could believe it.

A few days later,
one of the judges said
she'd made a mistake:

'I only score the blows I see,' she said.
'But I didn't see them all.
His body was in the way.'

Lennox was angry,
but he knew the answer,
was to fight again.

The two men met again 10 months later
in November 1999.

Holyfield said he'd knock Lennox out
in round three.
He didn't.

Instead,
Lennox nearly knocked Holyfield out
in round five.

Then, in the sixth,
Lennox stood back
and dropped his gloves.
He was saying to Holyfield –
there's no danger.
Come on! Fight!
Is that the best you can do?

By the end of the night,
Lennox was the clear winner.

At last, Lennox Lewis
held all three World Heavyweight titles!

6 Cool Champ

The US press don't like Lennox Lewis.
They don't like it
when a Brit beats all the US boxers.

They called him a garbage-can champion.
They called him grape juice,
pretending to be fine wine.

One man wrote:
'He says he loves his mother.
What kind of fighter says that?'

Lennox stays cool.

He saves his answers
for the boxing ring.

In May 2000,
he met Michael Grant
in New York.

Grant was the new kid on the block.

Lennox knocked him down
twice in the first round.
Grant went down a third time
in round two.
The fight was over.

Lennox was awesome.

'I was shocked by Grant,'
he said later.
'He came in really gutsy, but . . .
Any guy who steps in front of me
is going to get knocked out!'

7 The Tyson Fight

In January 2002,
Lennox got his fight with Mike Tyson.
But it wasn't in the boxing ring.

The two men met in New York.
It was to tell the press
they were going to fight
later that year.
But Tyson couldn't wait.

He marched across to Lennox
and swung a punch.
Twenty men piled in,
trying to get Tyson under control.
They all scrapped for ten minutes.
Tyson bit Lennox on the foot.

As usual,
Lennox got his own back
in the best time and place.

They met in June 2002,
in Memphis, Tennessee.

Lennox soon was in control.
He won seven of the eight rounds,
and cut Tyson's eye badly in round 3.

Then, in round 8, he hit Tyson
with a killer right-handed punch.
Tyson went down,
and he didn't get up again.

Lennox stood over him,
looking down at the broken man,
flat-out on the canvas.
Then the referee pushed Lennox
back to his corner.

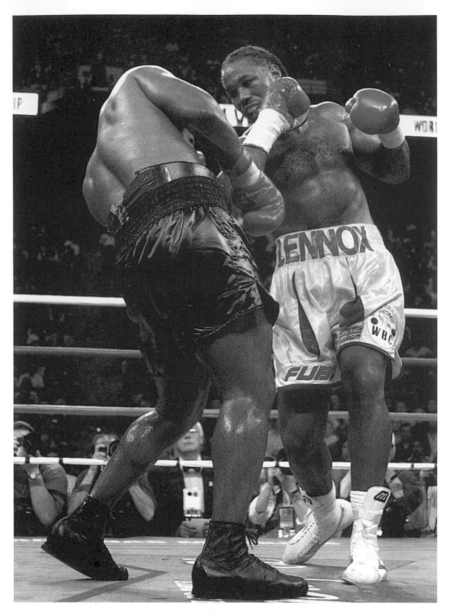

Lennox follows through on the punch that took
Mike Tyson down.

Later, Tyson gave Lennox respect:
'There was no way I could get to him.
He was just too big and too strong.'

Lennox was cool, as usual.
'I showed him the sweet science
of the sport,' he said.

But he added:
'I'm glad Tyson has eaten humble pie.'

Now people are saying that
Lennox is the greatest of all time.
He's come back from defeat
and he's knocked out the men
who once beat him.

Lennox might retire now.
After all, as he put it:
'I'm top of the food chain, now!'

But Mike Tyson wants to fight him again.
He needs to – he's $10 million in debt!

8 The Other Side of Lennox

What is he like outside the ring?

Lennox Lewis is not like other boxers.
He doesn't brag and boast.
He doesn't look punch-drunk,
or slur his words.

He has not got into trouble
with the police,
like Riddick Bowe
and Mike Tyson.

He is quiet, and shy.
He likes reading, and playing chess.

Here Lennox celebrates his win with his
mum and his manager, Frank Maloney.

He likes his mum's home cooking.
He takes her with him,
when he trains for a fight,
so she can cook for him.

When he's not training,
Lennox spends time in his three homes:
London, Canada, and Jamaica.

He can afford it.
Lennox has made over £80 million
since 1993!

Lennox put millions of pounds
into the Lennox Lewis College
in the East End of London.

The college aimed to help young people
to get a better start in life.
Many of the young people were in care.
Some were in trouble with the police.
Some had been excluded from school
(just like Lennox was).

'Young people want to learn,' says Lennox.
'They want to succeed.
They need support to get there.

'If I hadn't had support,
when I was young,
I would not be where I am today'

Today, the college is a boxing school
called the Lennox Lewis Centre.
Boxers from all over the world
come to train and study there.

Lennox Lewis training at the Lennox Lewis Centre.

'Boxing is not about hurting,'
Lennox has said.
'It's about not getting hurt.
That's the skill of it.'

You do what you have to
so you don't get hurt.

That's why Lennox will retire soon.
Quit while he's ahead.

He has houses all over the world.
He has all the money he needs.
He has a beautiful girlfriend named Aisha.
He's Heavyweight Champion of the World.

What else does he have to prove?

Well . . . there is always some young boxer
who wants to take a shot at the champion.

And there *is* that next fight against Mike Tyson . . .